A Beginners Guide to Dialectical Behavior Therapy

by William E Joyce

liable for any hardship or damages that may befall them after undertaking information described herein.

Additionally, the information in the following pages is intended only for informational purposes and should thus be thought of as universal. As befitting its nature, it is presented without assurance regarding its prolonged validity or interim quality. Trademarks that are mentioned are done without written consent and can in no way be considered an endorsement from the trademark holder.

Table of Contents

Introduction 1

Chapter 1: Dialectical behavior Therapy - What and Why?..... 3

Chapter 2: Building Willpower to Change 11

Chapter 3: Building Your Sense of Mindfulness.....................17

Chapter 4: Building Your Distress Tolerance 31

Chapter 5: Building Your Emotional Regulation................... 47

Chapter 6: Interpersonal Effectiveness................................ 55

Chapter 7: Helping Somebody Else.. 61

Conclusion 63

Introduction

Congratulations on downloading *Dialectical Behavior Therapy* and thank you for doing so.

The following chapters will discuss using dialectical behavior therapy in order to treat unstable moods, borderline personality disorder, and related complications. This book is intended to be used as a companion in addition to a personal therapist but can be used on its own as a general reference.

There are plenty of books on this subject on the market, thanks again for choosing this one! Every effort was made to ensure it is full of as much useful information as possible, please enjoy!

Chapter 1:
Dialectical behavior Therapy - What and Why?

We'll start this book out by asking a question which is central to the entire text: what is dialectical behavior therapy, and what benefits are there to using it? We're also going to be taking a look at some other important things, such as what distinguishes dialectical behavior therapy from other popular forms of therapy such as cognitive behavior therapy.

Where does dialectical behavior therapy's history lie? The story starts in the 1980s with a disorder called *borderline personality disorder.*

Borderline personality disorder is also known as *emotionally unstable personality disorder*, which tells you more or less a lot of what you need to know about the disorder. It can best be described as a long-recurring and deeply ingrained set of characteristics that revolve around a central feeling of emptiness and detachment, as well as a general fear of being abandoned.

People who suffer from borderline personality also tend to have a very unstable view of themselves and unstable emotions in general. People who suffer from borderline personality disorder often will have a parallel problem, such as a history of substance abuse, depression, or eating disorders like anorexia or bulimia. What's more is that people who have borderline personality disorder are relatively likely to die by suicide; in fact, one in ten people with borderline personality disorder will die by their own hand.

The most difficult part for treating people with borderline personality disorder was the fact that personality disorders tend to be very difficult to treat with medicine; their causes are not concrete and it's difficult to pin them down to a singular cause that medicine can be made to treat. It's more difficult, too, when you consider the fact that while other disorders usually have clear effects on the brain, borderline personality disorder *has* no such clear effect on the brain that can be easily mitigated by medicine. While there is evidence that it affects a certain *part* of the brain, there's no known method to really influence the exact cause of borderline personality disorder in any effective way. Medication can only really be prescribed to assuage periphery conditions but can't really influence the core condition in any sort of meaningful way.

In response to this, Dr. Marsha Linehan began to work on a form of treatment that was based off of the already extant *cognitive behavior therapy*. The treatment would become known as *dialectical behavior therapy*, and the intent was to take the concepts that existed already in cognitive behavior therapy and then institute new concepts that were brought over largely from Buddhist practice.

What resulted was the first form of psychotherapy proven to be generally effective in the treatment of borderline personality disorder. However, it's also proven useful in the treatment of people with general issues like self-harming or suicidal thoughts.

This specific variant of therapy works for these people in a way that most other forms of therapy do not because it is based around getting the patients to increase their ability to regulate both their emotions and their thoughts through assessing what actually causes them to feel the way they do, and what it is that they can do in order to apply it to themselves.

It does such through a collection of different concepts intended to isolate, analyze, and ignore negative thoughts entirely. To do so, dialectical behavior therapy is categorized into four distinct modules that are performed in a cyclical manner. These are as follows.

The first is *mindfulness*. Mindfulness is probably the most important building block of dialectical behavior therapy, and it is the thing which precludes everything else. Building mindfulness is absolutely essential. We'll be talking about mindfulness very in-depth in its respective chapter.

The second is *distress tolerance*. Distress tolerance refers largely to one's ability to deal with things that distress them. This runs in opposition to the current trend in mental health treatments to attempt to change stressful situations. For people with irrational or self-destructive thought patterns, the attempt to change these distressing situations may be one of the things which catalyze and worsen somebody's negative behaviors.

The third is *emotional regulation*. Emotional regulation deals with the ability for somebody to be able to recognize and handle their emotions reactively, as well as to deal with things with a greater level of detachment and objectivity. There are many different processes involved in the building of emotional regulation skills.

The last is *interpersonal effectiveness.* Interpersonal effectiveness has to do with the ability of an individual to effectively communicate and deal with other people. While people who suffer from borderline personality disorder and related problems generally are able to describe how a situation should be handled, they are usually unable to do so when they are in the driver's seat, so to speak. They will clam up or resort to knee-jerk reactions in dealing with other people.

It is through the cycling of these four concepts that one may receive the full benefits of dialectical behavior therapy.

The center of dialectical behavior therapy is based around the interaction between the therapist and the patient. The therapist is supposed to be highly supportive of the patient, being accessible outside of therapy sessions if necessary in order to provide constant emotional support for the patient. The patient is also intended to view the therapist as a friend rather than foe. In order to make this happen, the intent of the therapist is to accept the patient's feelings while also telling them that some of the things they do are negative and giving them guidance as to how they could deal with things in a better way.

The end goal of the sessions is for the patient to achieve what they would define as a "life worth living" through both the changing of current behaviors and the development of new behaviors.

So, with all of that in mind, one has to ask: with the focus of dialectical behavior therapy being so heavily geared towards the establishment of a relationship between a person and a therapist, is it a realistic approach to try to do it on your own?

The simple answer is that yes, it's realistic. However, it is going to take a lot of work on your end. By the end, though, you should be able to use dialectical behavior therapy in order to better manage your relationships, disorders, and general malaise.

The purpose of this book is to give you the necessary structure so that you're able to do dialectical behavior therapy on your own; however, there is a chapter reserved for helping somebody else using the method's in this book, such that you can act as their "therapist" as it were. Be aware that if you're going to do such a thing, you need to be mentally prepared for whatever the patient may throw at you. You have to truly be accepting of them, or they may not feel as if they have a friend in the process. The worst case is that you actually delay their progress. This is the last thing that you want to do!

The Outline for Dialectical Behavior Therapy

So now it's come time; you understand what dialectical behavior therapy is and you've decided that it's the best course of action for you. What can you start doing in order to get the most out of this system? What steps can you take in order to start integrating dialectical behavior therapy into your daily life?

The first thing you need to understand is that dialectical behavior therapy doesn't try to push everything on you at once. Rather, the method is based around periods where a certain one of the four methodologies behind dialectical behavior therapy are practiced.

It is, in total, a six-month program. This program may then be repeated over a long period of time until the patient feels comfortable using and maintaining the skills that they've developed.

One may separate the program into three distinct two-month blocks. All of these blocks start out with a two-week emphasis on mindfulness and mindfulness building techniques. The skills developed during the other periods should be maintained but should not be the absolute focus. There is a six week focus period after every two-week mindfulness session which will focus on one of the three other facets of dialectical behavior therapy depending upon the current block of the program.

The first block is based around the emotional regulation skill and will deal with building the skills which the patient most needs in order to effectively regulate their emotions.

The second block is based around the skill of tolerating distress and will deal with asserting and developing the patient's ability to tolerate distress. This block is extremely important to the development of the patient and is a major part of the whole process.

The third block is based around building the patient's ability to effectively communicate themselves to other people and maintain their interpersonal relationships. This block is supposed to build stability within the patient's environment and is also critical.

As the patient, you should place emphasis on being able to effectively navigate all of these skills. If you're working with someone else, you need to be checking in and making sure that you are blocking out and maintaining focus on each of these skills individually.

Managing the progression through each of these skills through the development of an effective timetable is highly important to the overall progress of whoever is trying to benefit from the therapy method; all of the parts are of great importance and priority must be placed on acting out all of them.

In each of the following chapters, we're going to be discussing the actions that you can take in order to practice all of these when the time comes and build your skills in general. Much of this is most easily accomplished with either a trained therapist or somebody who is willing to stick by your side as you try to do everything within this guide. However, it is very realistic that you are able to carry it out on your own so long as you build the self-discipline necessary to do so.

Chapter 2:
Building Willpower to Change

One thing that can be rather difficult when trying to make a positive change for yourself is actually taking the first step forward. Once you *do* take the first step and start to establish some sort of routine for yourself, you settle into it mentally and it becomes a lot easier. It also tends to become even easier as you press forward with it. However, when you're just starting out, it can be difficult to really cement that will within yourself.

Understand that the conduit to real and actionable change springs forth from within yourself. In fact, when working with people through the dialectical behavior method, therapists recognize that the first step is to make sure that the patient is agreeable and *wants* to get better.

Do understand that this book has a chapter dedicated to the idea of working with somebody else through dialectical behavior therapy, so if you're trying to work with somebody that you know and care about, this book does provide for you. However, the first several chapters are more based around the idea of working with *yourself.*

So, with all of that in mind, how can you take the first steps towards recognizing that something needs to change? The first is through an honest analysis of your actions and your behaviors.

The first thing you need to realize is that if there is constant tension in your life, there is a chance that you are a common denominator. There is nothing wrong with realizing this, though. We all carry a large amount of baggage throughout our lives and realizing how that baggage continues to affect you is a rather large part of the healing process.

Recognize that there is nothing wrong with wanting to change for the better. Healthiness is a good thing. You should be actively seeking this healthiness. Although it may not seem like it right now, the type of happiness that you're wanting is both real and attainable for everybody, even yourself.

The first step to getting there, though, is to admit to yourself that you need to change. If you recognize that things are going poorly, you need to analyze the things that are happening to you and honestly try to see what part you're playing in them.

Many people feel like the second that they admit to themselves that they could make a change, their entire life will be thrown out of whack. Sometimes they feel like their current life is too cemented to really make an effective change possible. Both of these viewpoints are explicitly wrong, though.

The truth is that while some major shifts might be necessary in your life in order for you to become a happier and healthier human, the vast majority of these are going to be coming from within yourself - they are not, necessarily, things which occur around you.

I suppose that the best part about it all is that most of the change comes from a shift in your general perspective. The weight that is lifted when you start to move away from those things which fog your general perception, in such a way that you can start to think and act rationally, is a very beautiful thing; you'll feel like a new person.

The biggest part of all of this comes with truly desiring to make a change. Understand that having that true desire for change means necessarily that you are able to accept things about yourself, even the hard things, that are generally difficult for you to accept.

These things may be good or bad, too; for example, if you suffer from depression, it may be that you need to accept that some of the irrational thoughts and conceptions aren't necessarily true. On the other hand, if you suffer from a bit of situational narcissism and tend to displace blame as a defense mechanism, you may find that you need to accept that you can, in fact, do wrong - even if your narcissism is a defense mechanism within itself.

The hardest part of all of this is the fact that mental illness really, ultimately, is not cut and dry. Working with mental illness can prove very difficult in fact, because everybody's mental illness will manifest in a way which is essentially different, even if the illnesses follow similar paths and share certain attributes. Therefore, it can be quite difficult to really get out of these rhythms and figure out what is true and isn't, as well as what will work for you and what won't.

Be aware, though, that all of the change you need will ultimately be summoned from within yourself. You must summon the desire to make a real and genuine effort to change.

You can and most likely will experience success using this method, but you have to be open to change. The big kicker is self-discipline. It's going to take a lot of self-discipline for you to navigate this form of therapy like you're going to need to.

When you suffer from the problems that dialectical behavior therapy is intended to fix, training this amount of self-discipline can be rather difficult in and of itself. It is not, however, impossible. Your mind is constantly frayed or jumping all over the place, or sometimes you have rapid and unbearable mood swings. Even if not those, it's possible that you react to situations in self-destructive ways that you don't quite understand. Perhaps you don't even know what you do or why, but you know that it's having a negative effect on your relationships.

The point of dialectical behavior therapy is ultimately to help you pinpoint, recognize, and then effect change in regard to these problems. In order to do so, you also have to be willing to admit to yourself that these problems exist in the first place. This is the crucial first step to progress. Understand this before you take any further action; reaching the end of the road to success requires that you drive it properly. Driving it properly here means that you need to be prepared to accept that you are not perfect; you will make mistakes, you will have inappropriate or hurtful thought patterns, you will do things that you ought not do. Accepting that you'll do so is absolutely pivotal in the grand scheme of sorting out your mental issues.

Another critical thing is avoiding getting discouraged. Remember that this program specifically lasts for *six months* and is meant to be cyclical such that it can be repeated as necessary. Your results are not going to be instantaneous, and chances are that you're going to regress sometimes too. Your method for dealing with this needs to revolve around accepting the fact that not everything is going to move in a linear fashion.

Realize that you're going to mess up from time to time, and also that you're ultimately not going to make a heap of progress all at once. Consider it like losing weight. When you lose a lot of weight, it can be difficult to really ascertain how much weight you've *lost*, because you see yourself every day. The only time that such a thing really becomes apparent is if you compare yourself to an old picture or if somebody brings up the fact that you've lost weight.

It's much the same here. While a lot of the mental changes won't be immediately noticeable, the changes you make to your mindset as a whole will lead to the development of a far healthier general thought process over the long run.

Chapter 3:
Building Your Sense of Mindfulness

The first part of working with dialectical behavior therapy lies in training a certain core set of skills. These skills are going to be essential to your progress in the method as a whole. Working with dialectical behavior therapy on your own can be difficult, but with effort you can make most of the concepts happen for yourself.

The first concept you need to work on building is mindfulness. Mindfulness is a critical part of dialectical behavior therapy as well as building your ability to deal with harmful thoughts in general. So, what exactly is mindfulness?

In the development of dialectical behavior therapy, concepts were synthesized into one cohesive unit from around the whole world. Some of these concepts came from the East. One such concept is that of *mindfulness*. Mindfulness is a difficult concept to explain at first. It basically revolves around the idea of being present in the given moment.

In order to express mindfulness, it's perhaps easier to think about the way that your mind works at any given moment. Much of the time, you're not actively thinking about what is happening at the moment; often, you'll enter into a sort of autopilot mode. Upon entering this autopilot mode, you tend to firstly lose track of the thoughts that you *ought* to be having.

However, other thoughts tend to come to the forefront as well - you may start thinking about the past or worrying about the future.

This is a perfectly normal response, don't worry; everybody passes their time thinking about something other than the present unless they specifically train themselves not to. However, the Eastern religions were right in their assessment of this practice: it firstly is illogical, given that the only thing which may happen is the present, and it secondly is a conduit to unnecessary suffering.

Breaking this habit is important, though. People never really think about how silly it is to be thinking about anything other than the present.

More than that, though, mindfulness is important in training yourself to let thoughts come and go. The skill of recognizing a thought and then releasing that thought is extremely important to anybody wanting to take control of their thoughts. Much of the time, you will think something irrational and then start to latch onto that thought. Going against this grain and letting the thought be set free is critical to the entirety of dialectical behavior therapy as well as making forward progress as a person in general.

Mindfulness is the simple concept of being aware of your thoughts. There are a few different things that you can do in order to train it. We're going to start with looking at the concept a little bit more closely before we get into the training of mindfulness reflexes, though.

Why might mindfulness be necessary, and how might you benefit from it?

Mindfulness is necessary in building the ability to allow yourself to simultaneously accept the emotions that you feel whenever you try to disrupt whatever destructive habits you may have developed, as well as giving you the skill set necessary to move forward and allow the thoughts not to bother you as much as they normally would.

A big part of borderline personality disorder, as well as suicidal ideation, substance abuse, and numerous other disorders, lies in the trend of irrational reaction. This trend exists as a function of recognizing some sort of issue - whether real or imaginary - then responding in an irrational manner to that issue. Mindfulness is a part of allowing yourself to recognize what is and isn't rational, then address it in a responsible way.

If, for example, you find it especially difficult to accept that somebody isn't going to abandon you, then you may find the ability to focus on what you're doing at that given moment and acknowledge what you're feeling in a passive way without reacting to it especially useful.

Mindfulness in psychology is typically viewed as a thoroughfare for you to start to understand yourself and your reactions, as well as a means of simultaneously avoiding two specific trains of emotional response: either the *avoidance* of necessary emotion, or the *over analysis of* and *overreaction to* emotion. In either case, mindfulness allows you to be actively engaged with your emotions in a whole manner as well as to be actively disengaged from your emotions by placing yourself more in the sphere of the *real world* as opposed to isolating yourself in a sphere of negative emotion.

Indeed, a rather large part of dialectical behavior therapy lies in the attempt of the patient to rid themselves of emotional suffering to the greatest extent which they possibly can.

So, moving further, we're going to start talking about the development of mindfulness in the context of dialectical behavior therapy. Mindfulness is divided into two distinct categories: *what* skills and *how* skills. Both of these are intended to help the end user with understanding and carrying out mindfulness as it were.

What

The *whats* are focused around answer the question of what we're trying to do when engaging ourselves in mindfulness practice. What are the end goals? What are we actually trying to accomplish?

The first thing that we're trying to accomplish is the ability to *observe* our emotions as well as the things around us. In this capacity, mindfulness is intended to allow us to do so in a nonjudgmental and somewhat objective manner. That is to say that observation in the context of mindfulness should ideally be rather detached. If you feel especially close to your situation, then you're feeling a way that is necessarily counter to what should be your "goal" in mindfulness training and exploration.

This isn't to say that you should actively tune out, but that you should practice the art of seeing yourself in a more detached way. For example, in a situation where you might otherwise deflect blame onto somebody else as a knee-jerk reaction, try to take a step back and look at the situation objectively. What happened?

Mindfulness is helpful in allowing you to both observe the situation in an active and detached way as well as giving you the clarity of mind that you need in order to either deal with or accept the situation in a meaningful manner.

One core focus of dialectical behavior therapy lies in the concept of *accepting* difficult situations. Realize that in these sorts of situations, while you may have a minimal effect, there are many more aspects than just you at the heart of them. What this ultimately means is that regardless of whatever you may be trying to do or whatever you may think, there's only so much of a hand you can have in any particular thing. Moreover, resistance to your fears and your knee jerk reactions in these sorts of situations often only exacerbates the problem. Dialectical behavior therapy is based around willing yourself to *accept situations* rather than trying to change them.

Mindfulness is a key part of acceptance, because if you are being actively mindful, you are realizing that you are only able to change *that which you are able to change.* You are mindful of your hand in the situation as well as - more importantly - *your reaction to the situation.* While total passivity is unnecessary and could even be harmful, you need to realize that total reaction can be just as harmful if not even more, especially when you already tend to overreact and be unstable in the first place.

The creator of dialectical behavior therapy recommends that one develops what she called a *Teflon mind*, which is essentially the ability to let things and emotions happen without them sticking around in your thoughts. In this philosophy lies the crux of mindfulness: active participation in the moment rather than letting yourself get bogged down with unnecessary things.

Mindfulness can have many aspects, but from moment to moment, you need to become as aware as possible of those things that you perceive through your senses, with your senses being necessarily defined as *vision, feeling, hearing, tasting, and smelling.* Your goal is to take in as much as you possibly can from these sources and be fully aware of what is happening *in the present moment.*

The next important *what* of mindfulness is the ability to *describe.* Description is an absolutely necessary skill. You need to gain the ability to say the things that you are observing. It's here that description gains the largest part of its utility.

Description is not easy initially, especially because you're trying to describe things without passing judgment on them. Indeed, gaining the ability to describe things without explicitly passing judgment on them is of paramount importance in the pursuit of finally being able to be completely attuned to your environment and working within it. More than that, it's of immense importance to the end goal of being able to process your *own* emotions in a nonjudgmental manner.

Behaving nonjudgmentally is a skill all in itself, and it's something you're trying to really ingrain with the description skill. You may not be entirely clear on just what description means in this context; really it just refers to your ability to pick out the traits about the things that you notice around you or within you and then communicating them effectively in a nonjudgmental manner.

The effective usage of this skill can lead to a huge amount of progress being made in the other facets as well.

The last *what* of mindfulness rests in *participation*. Participation is about being completely active in the moment. If you are doing something, participation asks that you be completely focused and involved with that activity. This harkens back to the idea of mindfulness initially being a tool of Eastern philosophy to gain complete and absolute awareness of any given moment.

Note that mindfulness is *not* easy, and neither is the skill of participation and being aware. These are, in fact, things that you're going to have to train over time. Don't be frustrated if you find it difficult at first to stay completely and utterly focused on the tasks at hand. Just practice bringing yourself back to them in a mindful manner.

What things can you do in order to bring yourself back to the activity at hand? Good question! The best techniques for restoring your mindful position are those in which you focus on the world around you. If you find yourself losing focus, bring yourself to attention and think of the things which correspond to your five senses. Describe them internally. Once you've done so, you'll find that your point of focus is often restored and you'll most likely be able to return to your core focus to your activity at any given moment.

Remember to use the moment as your tool. This is one of the most important parts about participation and mindfulness in general. There will never be but that which *is*, even if that which *is* will necessarily impacted by the past and the future. Because of that, you can always use what *is* in order to bring yourself back to focusing on what *is*.

If you find your mind floating off when you're doing something, use your senses or other mindfulness techniques you read about or develop in order to bring yourself back to where you need to be.

Mindfulness is a discipline, like anything else. It's going to be hard for you to build up the ability to consistently rein in your focus and tackle one specific thing. However, just like any other discipline, the more you practice at it, the better you'll become at it.

How

Now that we've discussed the *what*s of mindfulness, it's time that we start to discuss the *how*s of mindfulness. These are the essential ways in which you must necessarily approach mindfulness such that you can begin to actively revise some of the toxic patterns you've developed so far in your life. Recognizing these essential *hows* will be fundamental for you moving forward as well.

These hows answer the question of how you're supposed to be approaching your mindfulness exercises. In that, when you're trying to perfect your mindfulness technique, these will prove incredibly fruitful in your endeavor.

The first *how* is *nonjudgmentally*, as in *I should approach mindfulness nonjudgmentally*. As we talked about earlier in this chapter, the nonjudgmental approach to mindfulness is essential. This is because it allows you to shed any habits of judgment that you already have.

Moreover, when you do need to communicate your thoughts, by putting them through a nonjudgmental filter, you enable yourself to assess things in a very objective manner, or at least objective within a certain bound.

Additionally, when you act nonjudgmentally, it makes you as a person far more agreeable. One of your problems may be to either tell yourself or somebody else something in such a way that it makes it come off in a negative manner and learning to control this is absolutely essential to continuing in your mindfulness journey.

More than that, when you work with mindfulness and you act nonjudgmentally, you reduce your chance of ruining your focus by getting caught up in your prejudgments or judgments of something. This means that you're more likely to stay focused and on task than you may be otherwise. This can make a pretty huge difference in your ability to actually carry out your mindfulness practice.

The second how is that you need to practice mindfulness *one-mindfully*. What this means is that you need to hone your ability to stay focused in on one thing instead of letting your focus slide from topic to topic aimlessly.

The principle goal of this how is that when you are as focused as you ought to be, you can ideally keep yourself from slipping into your emotions and will therefore have a far easier time regulating your emotions and staying completely rational instead of potentially acting irrational.

Keeping yourself of one mind and on one task means that you are able to better able to allow yourself to run without the hindrance of your emotional mind. Indeed, being able to escape the hindering presence of the emotional mind is considered to be a critical part of dialectical behavior therapy.

Maintaining your state of one-mind will become far easier as time goes on and you work with the concepts more and more. Just remember that you need to keep doing what you can in order to maintain it. It will grow over time, like a muscle. This also means that early on it will tire you out to keep your focus for as prolonged as you're wanting to. Don't worry, though, this is a normal response to the heightened amount of concentration.

The objective of all of this is to improve your concentration, don't forget. Concentration is an extremely crucial part of mindfulness and the ability to concentrate and control your mind is a likewise crucial part.

The final how is *effectively*, as in *You should practice mindfulness effectively*. In that, there is a lot of meaning carried. Essentially, the point is that there is no right way or wrong way to practice mindfulness for these purposes necessarily; there's no need to get caught up in some sort of pseudo-religious dogma about the right or wrong way to be mindful - there are actual religions for that.

Instead, this how is about recognizing that mindfulness means a lot of things to a lot of people; it has both a historical religious meaning, a psychological meaning, and a couple other meanings that it's taken over time. In the end, most of the meanings meet on the general definition of mindfulness even if the specific goals of that type of mindfulness differ.

In that, there isn't necessarily a wrong way to attain mindfulness. Rather, your focus should be on simply attaining it. Therefore, don't worry about doing the right or wrong thing. Just do what works and is effective; in essence, do what you *need* to in order to become mindful. This is the path forward for proper mindfulness.

The goal of mindfulness training is to simply give you the ability to be mindful in a holistic manner, such that you can be mindful in as genuine of a way possible. This will help you gain control of your thoughts and your reactions, as well as your general mood and stability.

Remember that you are actively fighting against the current, too. This part will never be necessarily easy because it's a little bit ingrained into you to be emotionally unstable or otherwise have some sort of issue that you need to address; recognize this and recognize that these issues very well may reach down to even the level of your genetics.

However, while it won't ever be easy or 100% effective, it will cause you success in the long run as you gain more power over your emotions and your reactions. For this reason, you need to remember that even if you don't see success 100%, you still are looking for success, and you're looking for it in much *smaller* portions than 100%. Seek out your ability specifically to remain mindful when things get difficult, as well as your ability to regain your focus when you lose it.

In other words, mindfulness is a marathon, not a sprint. You don't need to expect major progress. You just need to expect that you can make small strides, even if irregular, and that these strides will help you to better treat, assess, and deal with the problems that you're trying to treat in the first place.

With all of that out of the way, it's time that we start talking about how you actually build mindfulness. After all, we've spent a long time talking about how you should practice mindfulness and what you should do, but we haven't quite talked about how you can actually *build* the skill of mindfulness.

The method that I'm going to recommend in particular is *meditation*. Meditation has been used for millennia to build mindfulness skills. While it may seem a bit hokey at first, meditation has been proven in psychological contexts to have a net positive psychological effect on people who do it regularly.

There is a method to meditation, though. Actually, there are many. The best advice that I can give you is to go on YouTube and seek out guided mindfulness meditation videos. These will walk you through the process of developing your mindfulness and general sense of focus.

Meditation will be hard at first and may seem boring, but over time you'll gain a greater and greater appreciation for the practice itself as well as a greater ability to actually carry out meditation in the capacity that you need to for the amount of time that you need to. Stick with it, because this is how you build mindfulness.

Stay present, stay alert, and stay in the moment. This is the point of the mindfulness training.

Chapter 4:
Building Your Distress Tolerance

Distress tolerance is an extremely important skill and, unfortunately, it's one that many people with borderline personality disorder and related mood/emotional disorders seem to lack. This doesn't mean that all is lost, however. Much of your reactions to things comes from a combination of learned behaviors and the environment around you. By relearning your methodology for processing and handling emotions, you can actually start to rebuild your ability to tolerate distress.

Dialectical behavior therapy differs largely from other mainstream therapy methods in that it places a rather large emphasis on the ability of the person to handle distress, such as trauma, circumstance, and generally worrying events. In some cases, they may utterly lack the ability to rationalize in a healthy way *why* certain things are happening to them, as well as *why they are the way that they are.* Other therapy methods tend to place an emphasis on things such as asserting the problems or how one can have a proactive effect on them.

The reason that dialectical behavior therapy places an emphasis on accepting things rather than making a proactive change is because people who would be helped by dialectical behavior therapy are often the type to overcompensate when they try to assert problems in their life. They might have an emotional overreaction or any number of other issues in response to a given stimulus. This is in contrast to the normal response to overwhelming stimuli, which is to be confused and potentially stay stagnant until a clear course is given for them.

Because of this, a lot of focus is placed in dialectical behavior therapy on not allowing stressful stimuli to place an emotional burden on you. In other words, allowing it to not unsettle your waters too much.

The ability to deal with stressful conditions is absolutely paramount in the development of a happy and healthy way of life. You can't expect to be happy if you don't have a regular, efficient, and healthy way of dealing with emotional trauma and general distress. There's a relatively decent chance that the reason you're pursuing this course in the first place is because you have a hard time dealing with your emotions as they come.

We'll talk more about dealing with emotions in an explicit manner in the following chapter, though. This chapter is more about dealing with the situations which *create* the emotions. Therefore, the center of this chapter is going to be developing skills that are necessary for the emotional development of you as a person. If you follow the general guidelines outlined in this chapter, you're going to find yourself able to much more frequently deal with situations which challenge you emotionally in a responsible way.

The first part of this chapter comes in really accepting what is going on around you. We talked about this in the first chapter, but it becomes critically important here. Many people have the critical initial response to try to block out, change, or entirely reject the thing that is happening to or around them. This is innately an unhealthy response mechanism, and you need to try to avoid it as much as possible.

The thing you need to realize is that no matter how much you want it to, blocking out or trying to change a situation which is out of your hands often won't do anything to really change it. Sometimes, things happen. Accepting this isn't a quitter mentality; trying to *reject* it is a quitter mentality, because it means that you aren't up to the challenge that's in front of you.

Often, people develop this mentality of self-rejection as a response to other stimuli. To have that response of trying to change or reject a situation means that you don't think that you are cut out to stand up to the situation. Part of dialectical behavior therapy consists of thinking about what causes you to feel this way and how you can avoid those triggers.

The creator of dialectical behavior therapy has defined a number of methods by which you can start to practice different tracts which are useful in the development of skills for distress tolerance. You need to practice these as much as you can in your day to day life such that you can start to intuitively use them when the need arises.

Review these daily when you're in the distress tolerance block so that you can firmly cement them into your mind. Also try to carry them with you in one way or another so that you can remember what steps to take when you need any of the given sets of actions.

The first set of actions that have been developed are methods of distraction. These are used so that when a distasteful emotion or situation comes up, you can start to distract yourself and divert your attention away from it in a productive manner. This will aid you in helping you to deal with emotional response. This also goes hand in hand with your mindfulness practice because the focusing ability that you develop when working with mindfulness will allow you to quickly draw your attention elsewhere and handle the things that are happening inside your head.

You can remember these actions through the acronym *ACCEPTS*. The letters in the acronym spell out a few different key ideas.

The first key idea is *activities*. When you need to distract yourself from something which is happening, try to divert your attention towards something else that you actually enjoy. This will take up your energy for a productive and positive emotional experience rather than one which will cause you to feel negatively and potentially even helpless.

The next key idea is *contribution*. Instead of focusing on yourself and the things happening to you in your immediate vicinity, focus instead on how you can help out others or the people around you. Use your time and resources and skills in order to make people around you feel better. This also has the additional benefit that it will make you feel like you're a better and more productive person than you did before, which will raise your level of productivity and your general feeling of self-worth. This has a reflexive benefit in that it starts to make you value yourself and feel slightly better.

The next key idea that you need to focus on building in the ACCEPTS distraction method is *comparisons*. Really, this idea is all about your perspective. Compare yourself both to how others are feeling in addition to the progress that you've made so far. While you are not in a great position at that moment, remember that some people out there are starving or homeless or worse. This isn't meant to condescend; it's meant to make you realize that as bad as things are, you are *not* at rock bottom. More important than that, though, is the ability to take inventory of your mental state and compare where you are to where you were. Since dialectical behavior therapy is about slow progression as a person, your entire goal is to build upon yourself over time. Recognizing that you've made progress can be a great way to make yourself feel like you're on the right track.

The following idea is *emotions*. This idea is about making yourself feel *other emotions* than what you're currently feeling. Watch or do something that makes you laugh or feel happy; participate in a hobby that makes you feel like you're in a different headspace than you normally do; do whatever you can in order to make yourself feel differently in general. This will give you the mental space that you need in order to put yourself in a better headspace.

After that, you need to practice *push away*. This idea is about being able to put your situation out of your mind for a while. This also goes hand in hand with your mindfulness practice. Being able to push things away from you in terms of your perspective is of paramount importance in being able to remain mindful and in control of your emotional reaction to different situations. While a situation may be far from apt or preferable, your ability to take that situation and push it out of your line of sight is going to be massively beneficial to you as you go forward.

The skill after that is *thoughts*. In essence, use the practice that you've developed in order to force yourself to think about something else. Clear your mental highway of traffic so that you can escape the jam, then cruise right on through in something that you feel comfortable and happy thinking about, or something that simply takes a lot of brain power and concentration for you.

The skill following this, and the final idea that you need to practice, is *sensation*. Sensations is about finding things that can make you feel different to how you do right now. These are things which have especially strong and visceral emotional reactions that you can't really resist. Try, for example, especially spicy snacks or very frigid showers. Both of these will allow your body to have a stress reaction to something else and will occupy your mind for a bit. The logic is essentially the same as pinching yourself when you stub your toe or hit your head so that you can divert your pain to something less painful. It's a real skill, and it's something that you need to develop. Plan for using this skill, because it can be especially useful to you.

Those ideas outline the central basis of the *accepts* distraction strategy. A bright idea would be to put them all on note cards and summarize them, then refresh yourself every morning when you wake up and every night before you go to bed when you're doing your distress tolerance block. These will help you in developing tolerance skills for distasteful or stressful situations.

Another thing that you need to focus on is finding a way to soothe yourself. This is a concept known as *self-soothing*, and it's especially important in dialectical behavior therapy.

Essentially, this is all about finding ways that you can be kind and comforting to yourself.

We aren't supposed to run all the time and never have an opportunity to destress. You are supposed to have periods of leisure time and simplicity. These are intended to help you with decompressing and unloading. Allowing yourself time to do this is important because it lets your mind reset to a bit of a blank state.

Many people who have extant emotional problems often experience that they're exacerbated by being in high stress environments and not allowing themselves the opportunity to really decompress and relax. While this won't solve all of your emotional problems at once, it can definitely help you in processing them when you're out and about. Remembering that you have the opportunity to destress at a later point in the day can also make it easier to take on the various stresses of any given day, too. Don't be afraid to set time aside for yourself.

What exactly should you be doing in this time? This is one of those things where the choice truly is yours. There is no right or wrong thing to be doing. Much like the final rule of meditation, the real goal here is just to be effective: do what works for you!

There are many different things that you may find soothes you. For example, give yourself time to take a bath at night, to read literature of your favorite genre, or to work on some sort of hobby or project. In effect, just be kind to yourself. Allow yourself the opportunity to relax. Know that there's nothing wrong with taking time to yourself. This is an important part of the distress tolerance block, so be sure to be incorporating it into your day to day.

The next most important concept is that of *making the moment the best it can be,* by following the IMPROVE acronym. This acronym is best used in order to improve the quality of moments that are particularly difficult for you. Remember to make as great of use of this as you can when you need to, and don't be afraid to write these things on note cards in order to remember them.

The first of these ideas is *imagery.* Imagery is about putting yourself in another place mentally. When things get particularly distressing, don't be afraid to think about something that *isn't* distressing. Imagine your favorite place, what it would be like if things were going the way you wanted them to, or just generally anything that makes you happy like your pet or your children. Putting yourself somewhere else in your mind can be very effective in making you feel like you're better equipped to deal with the situation at hand by allowing you to relax.

The next idea is *meaning.* Try to seek out a good reason for the emotion you're experiencing. In essence, if you're feeling a certain way, instead of rejecting your emotions subconsciously, allow yourself to think about why you're feeling the way that you are and what purpose it serves.

After that comes *prayer.* Do note that prayer doesn't necessarily have to be religious in nature. There are a lot of studies that have shown that simple recitation of something calming has the same subconscious relaxation effects as prayer does. The thing that you're actually benefiting from is releasing steam and finding tranquility in something, whether it be a phrase or a deity. In that, if you don't specifically worship somebody you could pray to, come up with a personal mantra you can say in order to make yourself feel better. If you do have somebody you pray to, then take the opportunity to speak to them about your situation; it will make you feel like you're more able to accept and deal with it.

Next in the *improve* set comes *relaxation*. Relaxation is exactly what it sounds like. Take the chance to just relax your muscles and use some of your self-soothing tactics so that you can become generally calmer and more ready to accept the given moment. Also, let's be honest: when you're tense and feeling generally out of it, you're not going to be at your best in terms of rationality. You should be staying as relaxed as possible at all times in order to ensure that you aren't going to have an irrational reaction to something.

After that comes *one*. This is about being able to focus on a singular thing. We keep coming back to this point because it's important to stress the ability to keep yourself moving moment to moment and not get caught up in things that you can't necessarily control. This will allow you to stay focused, not lose your train of thought, and continue to assess things as they are. In combination with your mindfulness training to look at things in a nonjudgmental way, this actually becomes one of the most powerful tools in your arsenal. You'll slowly gain the ability to look at things through a far healthier lens than you could before.

Next comes *vacation*. Vacation is all about letting yourself take a break from whatever you're doing, perhaps even a real vacation. Keep it brief, though, or else you'll lose steam.

However, it's very stressful on your mind to try to keep it in check all of the time. Don't let it focus on whatever is stressing you out; let it drift from topic to topic in a carefree manner while you let the world around you pass you by for a little bit.

Last, and this is most certainly not least - in fact, it's one of the most important things in the book that we haven't quite covered yet - is *encouraging yourself.* This is a fundamental skill to develop in dealing with inconsistent emotions and irregular reactions. The fact is that if you are having to read this at all, you feel to some level like you aren't fully able to deal with some of the things that happen in life. This may be due to early trauma, genetics, your environment growing up, your current environment, or any combination of things really. This means ultimately that you constantly have a voice inside your head telling you that you can't do it.

I'm going to digress for a moment, to be real and truthful with you. The fact is that most people who practice dialectical behavior therapy do so because they have borderline personality disorder. When people have borderline personality disorder, their prognosis isn't exactly great. While it's largely treatable with adequate therapy and possibly supplemental medication to aid with depression, ten percent of people with borderline personality disorder will end up killing themselves. This is a tragic and terrifying number.

If you are reading this because you have borderline personality disorder, or you read about it and think that you may fit the bill, I'd like to refer you to seeking the help of a medical professional who can be there in person with you and talk you through the various different options. Depression is real, it is heavy, and borderline personality disorder is constantly comorbid with it. While everybody can benefit from the skills that are developed through dialectical behavior therapy, if you're here because you fear that you might have borderline personality disorder, seek genuine help and get into a program with a personal therapist so that you can be sure you're getting the best and most personalized experience possible.

The reason that this is relevant and not a total digression is that sometimes, the ability to encourage yourself is going to be very, very difficult to maintain. In fact, if you do have depression comorbid with your mood or personality disorder, the chances are good that when I say you need to cheer yourself on, you have no idea what I'm even talking about. While it's easy to say from a certain perspective that you ideally should tell yourself that you can do anything, it's not the reality of the situation that just because you do it, you're going to believe it.

At first, when you tell yourself that you can do it, you're likely not even going to have an emotional kickback reaction; you're going to ask yourself, "what if I can't? why *would* I be able to do it?" and this is a tragic starting point. But even if you don't believe it, you need to fake it until you make it.

There are a lot of reasons that this is generally helpful. Your brain accepts what it's given ultimately, and if you say that you can do something, it's going to over time believe that it can. What you say and do is a very powerful emotional input, and recent psychological studies have shown that faking it until you make it is a very real phenomenon in terms of your brain structure.

More than that, the very act of telling yourself that you can do it, and accept whatever is happening, and cope with it properly, is extremely powerful. It's a psychological sword, if you will. If you do this, you can build the skill to accept what is coming your way and really work your way through it all, no matter what it may be. Telling yourself that you can do it is impactful.

Beyond all of that, over time you're going to develop the ability to believe yourself, because the simple fact that you *are* going to make it through everything that you're trying to do. While you may not believe it, you will always be able to ultimately cope with whatever you're trying to do. Think of it this way: all of life follows the same pattern. They are either moving forward, or they are at rock bottom, and rock bottom implicates dying. If you aren't dying, then you're progressing still. Find security in that fact. Your mind is designed to deal with various things, though it may not be designed to deal with them immediately. *Your* mind especially has a difficult time with this, because for one reason or another your brain has become wired to deal with things in an unhealthy manner.

However, that doesn't mean you can't undo this, and more importantly, the point of all of this is that hard things are, well, hard. You're going to have to work to get through them, and unfortunately that's just the nature of the beast. However, if you bear that in mind and ultimately work on accepting that fact, then you'll start to realize with time that when you tell yourself you *can* deal with something, that you ultimately *do*. This will reinforce the statement.

The statement also serves to make you more resilient to whatever may happen to you. For example, if you tell yourself that you *can* deal with things constantly, if things *do* get worse or if another bad thing does happen, you'll remember that you're able to deal with them whenever they do come up. Ultimately, you'll remember that the power absolutely lies within you to make what needs to happen, happen. This is your most powerful tool - your ability to encourage yourself and remember that whatever it takes, you *can* do it.

That brings an end to the specific *improve* set. As I said earlier, try to find a way to work these into your daily routine while you're doing the distress tolerance block so that you can remember them better when the time comes. Also consider setting them up in such a way that you can see them whenever you most find yourself needing them. This can be something as simple as writing them down in a notes app on your phone and summarizing them so that they're within easy reach, or even taking a screenshot of the pages that they're written on if you're reading this on something like a Kindle or Books app.

The next big part of distress tolerance is the ability to evaluate the pros and cons of something. Think about your given situation and think about what positives and negatives can come from it if you decide *not* to tolerate the situation. Is there any real and proactive change that you can initiate?

A lot of the time, when you're trying actively not to do something, there will be a kickback response in your mind that will manifest until you respond to it. (Unless you have OCD, in which case this is most likely a compulsion and you should avoid meditating on it.) Until you satisfy the answer of what would happen if you *did* respond to a situation - and analyze such in a realistic manner - you aren't going to feel comfortable with *not* responding to the situation. This shouldn't happen all the time, as it's a bad habit to ingrain, but when you do have the kickback response it's not a bad thing to think objectively about what would and wouldn't happen if you did decide to respond to the given stimulus.

Another thing that you need to practice is the concept of *total acceptance*. The truth is that a lot of the time, you're trying to actively fight against the reality of a situation. Sometimes, this is because you feel like you can't handle it. Other times, it's because you don't want to lapse control of the situation. In these sorts of situations, what you ultimately need to do is allow yourself to completely and total accept whatever is happening to you.

The fact is that you aren't going to change a reality that you *can't* change, no matter how much you try. Focusing on your inability to change it will only prove frustrating. There are some things that you only have so much of a hand in. In these cases, you can only do as much as you are able to do, and no amount of your action will change it.

Consider, for example, an illness in the family. What could you really do to change this stressful situation? Can you take away their illness? Can you fight against this tide? No, unfortunately. The sad truth is that you cannot. And while it's painful, the only thing that you can do which is healthy is to accept whatever might happen as something that you aren't able to change.

This should be practiced in tandem with your mindfulness strategies and your willpower such that you're able to practice the next skill: *turning your mind*. The objective of this skill is working on your ability to make yourself accept what is happening instead of rejecting it. One of the major problems in issues like borderline personality disorder is that you develop a personality which of its very nature has a very difficult time accepting whatever is happening. Your knee-jerk reaction is to reject whatever is happening because it means lapsing control of the situation or being powerless.

You need to work on honing that skill so that you can start to accept whatever may happen. You need to practice your ability to make yourself accept things. Acceptance is a habit, and while you shouldn't accept *everything* which passes, you must learn to accept those things which you have no hand in. Any other reaction is irrational, as there was little that you could have done to change it. While you can fight with yourself over what this phrase really means and whether or not you can do anything to change something, the simplest answer is the correct one: often, you can't.

Building the habit of acceptance will shift you toward a generally healthier state of mind that will let you start to work with things and concepts in a far better way than you are right now. You'll be able to process your emotions in a better way.

All of these skills culminate in the last skill of distress tolerance which is to learn the difference between being *willing to do something* and being *excessively willful*. *Willingness* is the will to do that which can actually have an effect. For example, if you don't like how much you make and you can financially afford to go and get another degree, you should be *willing* to get a degree. Don't accept a bad lot in life just because you develop an acceptance stance. *Willfulness* is the will to do something which *can't* have an effect; in essence, willfulness is being excessively willful to the point that you want to change things that you cannot. In these cases, your willfulness is breaking from your ability to be accepting of the things you cannot change, which causes unnecessary inner tension. You have to release that tension and allow yourself to accept that which you cannot change. In that, you will find your place in life becoming happier and your way of looking at life becoming healthier. You will no longer obsess over changing things you cannot, but you will find yourself being more willing to do those things which are *effective.*

That all brings the chapter on distress tolerance to the end. All of these skills should be practiced during your distress tolerance block. There were a lot of acronyms that you needed to practice and retain, so try to get to work on doing that so that you can remember these in your day to day life.

The important thing to note about your blocks, if you haven't already, is that you need to be carrying these skills into your day-to-day life even outside of their designated block; the designated block is merely intended to give you a time for extended focus on a given subject so that you can train those methods and start working on retaining them.

If you're reading through this book at once and thinking that you should try to implement all of these things at once, I'd like to warn you not to; your therapy will be more ineffective. Your brain isn't set up to deal with that much change at once. Remember that this is a marathon and not a sprint, just like I said earlier; your success with these methods is highly dependent upon your ability to retain these things and use them actionably. Carry them with you, but don't load them all on yourself at once.

Chapter 5:
Building Your Emotional Regulation

At this point in the game, we reach the second to last major skill that you're trying to train through these dialectical behavior therapy techniques. This is emotional regulation.

Note that all of these skills intertwine with one another in a very necessary way. Mindfulness, for example, gives you the ability to treat distress tolerance and emotional regulation with the detachment that they deserve; distress tolerance gives you an important base for regulating your emotions when times get especially difficult; and emotional regulation builds on mindfulness skills and distress tolerance skills in order to allow you to regulate your emotions to the greatest extent possible. Interpersonal effectiveness is about working on your ability to make your conversations with others more effective in reference to the things we've already talked about.

So, what is emotional regulation, and what is the reason behind it? Well, to answer the first question, emotional regulation is relatively self-explanatory. It's a set of different procedures and systems that have been developed in order to help people who have difficulties controlling their emotions in a more consistent, regular, and healthy way.

Ultimately, it's just the idea of metering your negative and harmful emotions in such a way that you can become a better person all around and deal with various different problems in a more conducive way. It also allows you to build a better sense of detachment and acceptance from your problems so that you can better isolate their root causes and figure out what you could be doing in order to better help yourself.

This is important to people who are suffering from things like borderline personality disorder or who are suicidal or otherwise emotionally unstable because they tend to have unpredictable and intense emotions; for example, you might feel angry, depressed, anxious, or inexplicably annoyed. While these things are appropriate and understandable emotions in a variety of different cases - completely blocking out your emotions is just as unhealthy as having too intense of emotions - you need to learn to feel them at an emotionally healthy level and not allow them to become irregular or irrational.

The first skill that you need to do in order to regulate your emotions is to understand what emotions you're feeling and why you're feeling them. You can do this by breaking them down with what's called the *story of emotion*.

The story of emotion is a crucial skill in breaking down your emotions and knowing what exactly it is that you're feeling. Some emotions are particularly difficult to process, and you don't always feel just one emotion; often, you'll feel multiple at once in a very disconnected sort of way. What do you do in this kind of situation? Well, you break down multiple signals and think about what they might indicate that you're feeling.

The first thing you need to analyze is what exactly prompted what you're feeling. This can be a massive tell in whatever emotion you're experiencing. If somebody cuts in front of you in traffic, you might have cause to feel angry, for example.

The second thing you need to analyze is how you *interpreted* the event. What happened in your eyes, how did you take it in? What can you do in order to distance yourself from the event a little bit and analyze it with somewhat clearer eyes? All of this can have a massive effect on your reaction.

The third thing you need to analyze is what you're feeling in terms of your body. Do you have a pit of fire in your stomach? Does it feel like your stomach is churning? Our brain has all kinds of interesting ways of indicating to us that we're feeling a certain way about something. It's a very interesting sort of intertwining phenomenon between our brain and our body.

The fourth thing you have to analyze is how you're subconsciously reacting to the event. Are your arms crossed? Do you feel more emotionally closed off than you did prior to the event? Is your jaw or face tense, or are your eyes wider than normal? All of these sorts of things indicate different emotions.

The fifth thing that you have to analyze is what you feel the *urge* to do. If you feel the urge to ram into the back of somebody's car when they cut you off, the chance is good that you're feeling anger, for example. You can understand your emotions based off of the thing that they make you want to do.

The sixth thing that you have to understand is the action that you *took*. Did you curse when they cut you off, or flip them off?

This is yet another indicator that you are angry. These sorts of things tell you what you're feeling.

The last thing you need to analyze is the name of the emotion, taking into account all of the other things on the list. If you're feeling angry, recognize that you're feeling angry based off of the fact that you did angry things and had what you perceived as a reason to be angry.

There's a great amount of importance in all of this; while it may seem silly to *tell* yourself what you're feeling, it can be a fantastic tool for putting things into perspective and analyzing what you're feeling under the hood. It can also make you realize that you're feeling irrationally about something and that you need to take a step back if at all possible. Recognizing what you're feeling can do a lot in terms of metering what you're feeling.

The ultimate goal is to distance yourself from what is called the "emotion mind"; in doing this, you build your ability to recognize and adapt to things with your conscious and mindful thoughts rather than reacting in a visceral and nearly primal manner based off of whatever your wit and whimsy may be.

There are a number of things that you can do in terms of your physical health that will allow you better regulate your emotions. You can remember these through the acronym *PLEASE*.

The first thing in the *PLEASE* set is *Physical* health. Pay close attention to your physical health; if you are sick or hurt in some sort of way, you need to do what you can to get to a doctor and get it taken care of. When you're sick, you don't have as much energy as you normally would to maintain control of your mind.

The second thing in the set is proper *Eating* habits. This is about reviewing the manner in which you eat and ensuring that you're getting all of the nutrients that you need. Don't eat too much or too little and eat *proper* food if at all possible instead of junk food. Sometimes, finances get in the way of this; don't make the mistake of thinking that cheap food can't be healthy food, though. Things such as canned carrots and spinach, beans, rice, and so forth are all healthy staple foods that can be prepared in numerous different ways and that pack a ton of nutrients.

The third thing is *avoidance* of drugs. Essentially, drop all things that you can which alter your mood. This is often a big deal for people who suffer from things like borderline personality disorder because they tend to have high rates of substance abuse as well. This isn't me trying to be D.A.R.E., this is a genuine suggestion; drugs may make you feel better in the short time, but they have an overall unpredictable impact on your long-term mood. Some people find therapy in certain things which can be prescribed, and that's alright. The concern is more with things like alcohol, opiates, and stimulants. Things of this nature can cause your moods to be unpredictable and more volatile than usual, especially due to their addictive potential.

The fourth thing is *sleeping* habits. Be sure that you're getting the proper amount of sleep. Try to get between seven and nine hours per night. More or less can throw your body's chemistry out of whack in pretty major ways, which will ruin your mood generally.

The final thing is *exercise*. Exercise is a cornerstone of both mental and physical health. In terms of physical health, you'll feel like you look better if you do a proper amount of exercise. In terms of mental health, exercise causes the release of endorphins and various chemicals in your brain which cause you to feel better and happier in general.

That brings an end to the *PLEASE* set. In addition to the *PLEASE* set, you need to work on building self-discipline through working on at least one thing every day. Try to end up mastering something. This will make you feel better about yourself and teach you a lot about self-discipline and self-control in addition to making you feel generally more competent.

A big cornerstone of this particular block of dialectical behavior therapy is that you are able to effectively use the concept of opposite action. Opposite action is used in order to curb your urges and do and feel the "right" thing when you have an emotion which is difficult to justify. Through emotional reflection and detachment, you should be able to realize when it's right or wrong to feel an emotion. If you feel something that you ideally shouldn't be feeling, use opposite action.

Opposite action is the idea that you do whatever is the exact opposite of the urges that you're having in that given moment. This is used for unhealthy and self-destructive emotions like unjustified anger or annoyance. Instead of doing whatever the emotion makes you feel specifically compelled to do in that moment, do whatever is the polar opposite of that.

This in effect causes you to leave the emotion you aren't wanting behind by instead feeling the emotion which is the exact opposite. While this does come across as a bit reductionist, the use of it is actually rather intuitive and you'll likely find that it can help you to feel a lot better in emotionally volatile situations.

So, what if your emotion is justified? What can you do? This is the skill of *problem solving*. Detach yourself from the situation and see what you realistically are able to do in order to solve it. If you can't do anything, then accept the situation at hand and allow yourself to feel the emotion. If you can do something, then take reasonable, actionable, and effective steps forward in order to start ameliorating the situation which is troubling you.

The last key concept of emotional regulation goes hand in hand with the acceptance and mindfulness topics that we've discussed already. This is letting go of your emotions. The idea, as I said earlier, isn't to block out your emotions entirely but rather to feel them in a rational and relatively healthy way.

Think about the emotion that you're feeling; give it genuine thought and accept that whatever it is, it's happening. Acceptance of an emotion does not necessarily mean reaction to it; it simply means that you acknowledge that the emotion is occurring. Once you've done so, you can simply let the emotion pass over you.

Using all of these skills together, you have a very good base for emotional regulation. Remember, you're trying to make yourself happier and build a life worth living. You can only do that by learning to have discipline in terms of your day-to-day emotions and letting yourself feel in a healthy way.

54

Chapter 6: Interpersonal Effectiveness

The final specific skill that you're trying to build through dialectical behavior therapy is *interpersonal effectiveness*. Interpersonal effectiveness is used in order to allow you to assert yourself effectively, deal with conflict, and deal with people in a polite and empathetic way.

The trouble for many people with dialectical behavior therapy is that they find it difficult to apply their generally good interpersonal skills to a conversation that they're actively having.

The first thing that you need to practice with is your ability to convey your emotions and desires to somebody else. This is all intended to help you effectively get what you need whenever you do need something. You can do is using the acronym *DEEAR MAN*.

D stands for *describe*, referring to you describing the situation that you're in as objectively and nonjudgmentally as possible, using your mindfulness skills to detach from it.

E stands for *express*, referring to your ability to tell them how you felt when the situation happened, what causes this to be an issue for you, and how you currently feel regarding the situation.

The second E stands for *empathy*; take into account what they're feeling and what they've experienced. This is important in creating an equal emotional playing field and being able to ask for whatever it is that you're asking for.

A stands for *assert*, referring to your ability to express what you want in a very clear and specific manner.

R stands for *reinforce;* offer a positive reinforcement if they should do what you're wanting them to do.

M stands for *mindful*; remain as mindful of the situation as possible, staying focused on the thing that you want and moving the conversation back to that pertinent topic if the other person moves away from it.

A stands for *appear*, referring to how you project yourself. Project confidence even though you may not actually be confident.

N stands for *negotiate*, referring to the fact that if somebody is hesitant, come to a compromise with them after asserting yourself clearly so that you two may be on the same page.

Using these skills, you will be able to more assertively and effectively ask somebody for something; this skill is very important in developing your ability to be more demanding and stand up for yourself.

The second set of skills is intended to help you with maintaining your relationships and make people feel open towards you. They are essentially to help you radiate warmth and overall be a more enjoyable person to be around. They can be remembered using the acronym *GIVE*.

The first letter, G, refers to *gentleness*: be gentle with the person in question, don't be judgmental, overall just be a good person using language which is fit for the situation. Don't cut the person down and always be courteous. Good-natured joking is alright so long as the other person is okay with it, and sarcasm should be avoided unless they've made it clear that they're okay with it.

The second letter, I, refers to *interest*: show the person that you're interested by acting interested. Don't avert your eyes, ask them questions whenever the moment is right, and avoid having any distractions out that may make it seem like you don't care about what they have to say.

The third letter, V, refers to *validation*: show that you understand what they're trying to say and what they're trying to communicate. Demonstrate that you can sympathize with them. You don't necessarily have to say it; you can express it through your body language and the way that you react facially.

The fourth letter, E, refers to *easiness*: have an easy disposition. Be as calm and relaxed as you can be, make them laugh, and remember to demonstrate that you're relaxed by smiling and not seeming like you're dire all the time.

Through the use of these different tips, you'll build an important repertoire for making yourself come off as caring, empathetic, and warm. This will foster relationships with people no matter who they are and make you come off as a good person to know and be around.

The last acronym, FAST, is based around your ability to maintain your position and know your value, not losing your sense of self-respect for anybody. This is critically important, because people with borderline personality disorder tend to invest too much of themselves into somebody else's opinion and will often change themselves for them. You can build your sense of self-respect and your opinion of yourself by sticking to it.

The *f* stands for *fair*: always be fair, both to yourself and to the person that you're talking to.

The *a* stands for *apologizing*: do apologize, but not too much. You have no reason to apologize more than once for something that you've done ineffectively. You shouldn't feel like you do.

The *s* stands for *staying*: stay true to your beliefs and your values. Don't let people tell you that you should be anything other than you are or feel anything other than you feel. This doesn't mean that you should bullheadedly reject anything that somebody tells you; you need to keep an open mind, of course, and if they have good reason to say you're wrong then consider the possibility that you may be. However, if they're just being mean or trying to get you to do something you normally wouldn't, respect yourself enough to stick to your guns.

The *t* stands for *truth*: never lie. Lies only build upon themselves, hurt your relationships, and eventually culminate in the damaging of your own sense of self-respect as well.

These are, in essence, the things you need to practice and keep in mind during your interpersonal effectiveness block. Carry them with you afterward as you progress further.

That brings an end to the specific skills that you need to practice in order to fully get the benefits of dialectical behavior therapy. If you pay close attention to them and try to follow the values, then you can come out the other end a stronger and happier person. The end goal is to build a life worth living, and I think that you can do it.

Chapter 7:
Helping Somebody Else

This chapter is going to focus on the things that you can do if you need to help somebody else who is trying to do dialectical behavior therapy.

The first thing that you need to understand is that you need to try to get them to go to a real therapist if possible. You may be kind and compassionate, but you are not trained. You cannot do all of this on your own, and you are not necessarily qualified to do dialectical behavior therapy. If you do try, though, there are a number of things that you should keep in mind.

The first is that a crux of dialectical behavior therapy as a therapist figure is that you validate their emotions, but tell them when they're doing something that's ineffective, ineffective meaning something which is self-destructive or potentially harmful to them.

You also need to make them feel like they can be as open as possible. Another reason that therapists can often be superior is that they have impartiality. While they do cost money, that money comes with a promise of experience, confidentiality, and qualification. Be as warm and receptive to them, but don't reinforce negative behaviors.

Ensure that they stay on track. Keep a record for them of the things that they do that inhibit their personal progress forward, like failing to keep a proper meditation routine. Go over this with them once a week and make them aware of the things they're doing ineffectively. Gently remind them that they aren't going to make progress if they don't make effort.

In essence, the best thing that you can do to help somebody else is to redirect them to somebody who is qualified to help. Understandably, though, sometimes that isn't an option. In this case, make yourself as warm and receptive to them as possible, let them be open, do whatever you can to ensure they keep respecting you - they obviously do, or they wouldn't ask you to help them with such sincerity in the first place.

It's a long and hard ride, and you have to expect to be able to pick up the phone if they need guidance at any point for at least six months. If you can do that, be accepting, be warm, and be impartial and objective, then you can maybe help them.

I genuinely wish you the best of luck if this is the path you have to take.

Conclusion

Thank for making it through to the end of *Dialectical Behavior Therapy*, let's hope it was informative and able to provide you with all of the tools you need to achieve your goals whatever it may be.

The next step is to get started on the path forward. Try to find a personal therapist if you don't have one, as they can really help you to reinforce these different practices and give you the impartial help that you need. If that's not in the outlook, then just get started on the path as soon as you can. Regardless of whether or not you have a personal therapist, the insights contained in this book can be hugely helpful in allowing you to develop a sense of emotional discipline and forwardness that you may desperately need.

Finally, if you found this book useful in anyway, a review on Amazon is always appreciated!

9 781718 909892